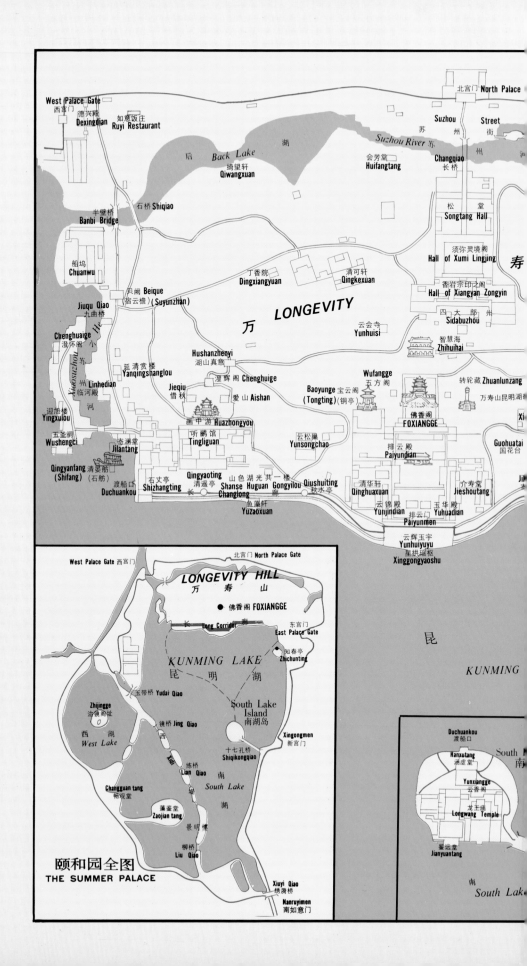

North Palace
北宫门

West Palace Gate
西宫门
德兴殿 Dexingdian
如意饭庄 Ruyi Restaurant

Suzhou
苏州
Street
街

Suzhou River 苏

后 湖
Back Lake
绮望轩 Qiwangxuan

会芳堂 Huifangtang

Changqiao
长桥

石桥 Shiqiao

松 堂 Songtang Hall

半壁桥 Banbi Bridge

须弥灵境阁 Hall of Xumi Lingjing

船坞 Chuanwu

丁香院 Dingxiangyuan

清可轩 Qingkexuan

香岩宗印之阁 Hall of Xiangyan Zongyin

寿

贝阙 Beique
(宿云檐)(Suyunzhan)

万 LONGEVITY

Jiuqu Qiao
九曲桥

四 大 部 州 Sidabuzhou

Chenghuaige
湛怀阁 小

云会寺 Yunhuisi

延清赏楼 Yanqingshanglou

湖山真意 Hushanzhenyi

智慧海 Zhihuihai

Linhedian
临河殿

澄辉阁 Chenghuige
Jieqiu 借秋

五方阁 Wufangge

转轮藏 Zhuanlunzang

Xiaosuzhou He

爱山 Aishan

宝云阁 Baoyunge (Tongting)(铜亭)

万寿山昆明湖

迎旭楼 Yingxulou

画中游 Huazhongyou

FOXIANGGE

五圣祠 Wushengci

听鹂馆 Tingliguan

云松巢 Yunsongchao

排云殿 Paiyundian

国花台 Guohuatai

念澄堂
Qingyanfang 清晏舫 Jilantang
(Shifang) (石舫)

石丈亭 Shizhangting

Qingyaoting
清遥亭

山色湖光共一楼 Shanse Huguan

秋水亭 Qiushuiting

清华轩 Qinghuaxuan

介寿堂 Jieshoutang

渡船口 Duchuankou

长 Changlong

鱼藻轩 Yuzaoxuan

Gongyilou

云锦殿 Yunjindian

玉华殿 Yuhuadian

排云门 Paiyunmen

云辉玉宇 Yunhuiyuyu
星拱瑶枢 Xinggongyaoshu

THE SUMMER PALACE
颐和园全图

West Palace Gate 西宫门
北宫门 North Palace Gate

LONGEVITY HILL
万 寿 山

佛香阁 FOXIANGGE

长 廊 Long Corridor
东宫门 East Palace Gate

KUNMING LAKE
昆 明 湖

知春亭 Zhichunting

昆

KUNMING

Zhijingge
治镜阁址

玉带桥 Yudai Qiao

South Lake Island
南湖岛

西 湖 West Lake

镜桥 Jing Qiao

新宫门 Xingongmen

西

十七孔桥 Shiqikongqiao

Duchuankou
渡船口

South

南

练桥 Lian Qiao

南

堤

Changguan tang
畅观堂

Hanxutang
涵虚堂

藻鉴堂 Zaojian tang

South Lake
湖

景明楼

Yunxiangge
云香阁

龙王庙 Longwang Temple

柳桥 Liu Qiao

Xiuyi Qiao
绣漪桥

鉴远堂 Jianyuantang

Nanruyimen
南如意门

南
South Lak

颐和园导游简图
GUIDE TO THE SUMMER PALACE

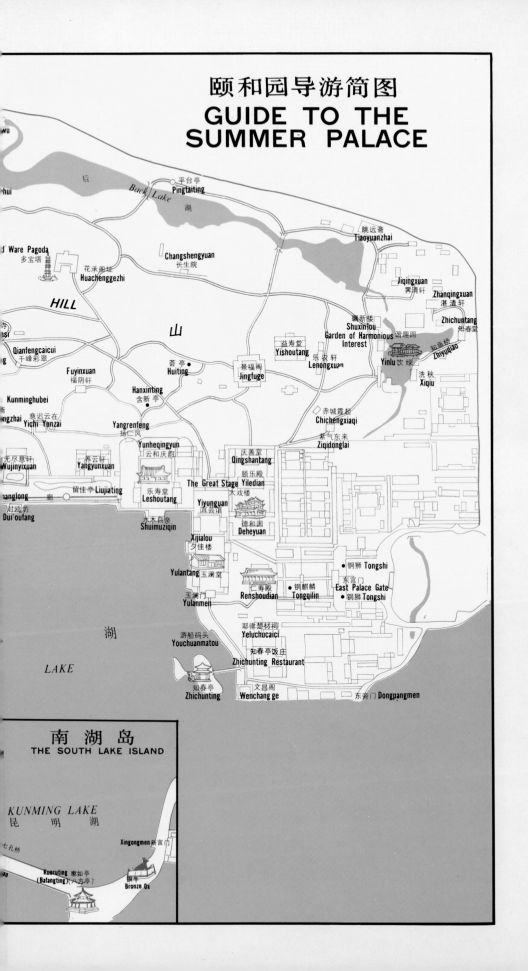

后 湖 *Back Lake*

平台亭 Pingtaiting

眺远斋 Tiaoyuanzhai

Ware Pagoda 多宝塔

花承阁址 Huachenggezhi

Changshengyuan 长生院

Jiqingxuan 霁清轩

Zhanqingxuan 湛清轩

Zhichuntang 知春堂

瞩新楼 Shuxinlou Garden of Harmonious Interest 谐趣园

HILL

山

si

Qianfengcaicui 千峰彩翠

益寿堂 Yishoutang

乐农轩 Lenongxuan

Yinlu 饮绿

知鱼桥 Zhiyuqiao

Fuyinxuan 福阴轩

荟亭 Huiting

景福阁 Jingfuge

洗秋 Xiqiu

Kunminghubei

Hanxinting 含新亭

gzhai 意迟云在 Yichi Yunzai

Yangrenfeng 扬仁风

赤城霞起 Chichengxiaqi

Wujinyixuan 无尽意轩 养云轩 Yangyunxuan

Yunheqingyun 云和庆韵

紫气东来 Ziqidonglai

庆善堂 Qingshantang

anglong 廊

留佳亭 Liujiating

颐乐殿 **The Great Stage** Yiledian

Dui'oufang 对鸥坊

乐寿堂 Leshoutang

Yiyunguan 宜芸馆 大戏楼

水木自亲 Shuimuziqin

Xijialou 夕佳楼

德和园 Deheyuan

铜狮 Tongshi

Yulantang 玉澜堂

仁寿殿 Renshoudian

铜麒麟 Tongqilin

东宫门 **East Palace Gate**

铜狮 Tongshi

玉澜门 Yulanmen

耶律楚材祠 Yeluchucaici

游船码头 Youchuanmatou

知春亭饭庄 Zhichunting Restaurant

湖 *LAKE*

知春亭 Zhichunting

文昌阁 Wenchang ge

东旁门 Dongpangmen

南湖岛
THE SOUTH LAKE ISLAND

KUNMING LAKE 昆明湖

七孔桥

Xingongmen 新宫门

Kuoruting 廓如亭 (Bafangting) 八方亭

铜牛 Bronze Ox

The Summer Palace

颐和园

溥杰

朝华出版社
MORNING GLORY PUBLISHERS

Second edition 2001

图书在版编目（ＣＬＰ）数据

颐和园／宇辰主编.—北京：朝华出版社，2001.6
ISBN 7-5054-0758-9

Ⅰ.颐...　Ⅱ.宇...　Ⅲ.颐和园-简介-汉、英
Ⅵ.k928.73

中国版本图书馆CIP数据核字（2001）第034880号

ISBN 7-5054-0758-9

Published dy the Morning Glory Publishers
35 Chegongzhuang Xilu, Beijing 100044 China
Distributed by China International Book Trading Corporation
35 Chegongzhuang Xilu, Beijing China
P. O. Box 399, Beijing, 100044 China

Printed in the People's Republic of China

目 录
CONTENTS

前 言

颐和园位于北京市西北郊，距市中心约15公里。它占地290多公顷，其中水面约220公顷。整个园区内有殿堂楼阁、亭台水榭3000余间，是清代（公元1644－1911年）末期帝、后政治活动和游憩的主要御园。

颐和园原名清漪园，主要由万寿山和昆明湖组成。万寿山为燕山支脉，高不足60米。十二世纪初，金代在此始建行宫，并引玉泉山水至万寿山下形成湖泊，把这里变为建造皇家苑囿的理想之地。

公元十六世纪至十九世纪中叶，是中国园林建筑空前发展的时期。尤其在十八世纪中叶，皇家园林的兴建进入鼎盛时期。乾隆皇帝（公元1736－1795年在位）在位的六十年间，仅在京城的西北郊由他亲自主持新建的大型园林就有五座。这就是著名的"三山五园"：畅春园、圆明园、香山静宜园、玉泉山静明园和万寿山清漪园（颐和园前身）。

公元1750年，乾隆皇帝为庆贺他生母孝圣皇太后的60大寿，下令动工兴建清漪园，全部工程进行了15年，其规模与现在的颐和园相当。那时的京城西北郊，极目所见，皆为绿树掩映、馆阁连绵的名园胜宫。这位对于"园林之乐，不能忘怀"的皇帝，六次下江南巡幸游览，把他看中的园林和名胜，均令随行的宫廷画师摹绘下来，作为建园的参考。造园匠师们在建造这些皇家园林时，不但继承了中国北方园林的雄浑气概，还融会了江南园林婉约多姿、柔美典雅的建筑特色，从而形成了中国园林艺术发展史上的高峰。

第二次鸦片战争时期，1860年英法联军攻入北京，"三山五园"被联军一把火烧毁。当时正是清代第七个皇帝咸丰（公元1851－1861年在位）当政，他带着后、妃逃到热河（今河北省承德市），次年病死热河行宫。咸丰皇帝的贵妃叶赫那拉氏（慈禧太后）在"垂帘听政"的名义下，独揽朝纲达48年，其间数度指使亲信奏请皇帝修复清漪、圆明诸园，因王公大臣异议，只好作罢。1875年光绪皇帝继位后，其父醇亲王主持海军事务衙门，为讨好慈禧太后，借口营建海军学堂，挪用海军军费，动工修复清漪园。偌大的工程，竟一直在暗中进行，直到1888年工程行将结束时，慈禧太后才以光绪皇帝名义发布"上谕"向外公开，并取"颐养冲和"之意，将清漪园改名为颐和园。1900年，八国联军侵入北京，慈禧太后出逃西安，颐和园再遭浩劫，文物珍宝被掠夺一空，建筑物再次遭到严重破坏。1902年慈禧太后回到北京，下令立即修复颐和园，次年完工。从此，她晚年的大部分时间在颐和园度过，一般是春二月进园，冬十一月才回紫禁城。

颐和园的建筑布局很特别，即在园区专门建造了一个宫廷区，在总体规划上，形成宫、苑分置的格局。慈禧太后晚年，大多在这里接见臣僚，处理朝政。宫廷区建筑物的所有屋顶都用朴素的青灰瓦代替华丽的琉璃瓦；庭院内广植长青树，点缀着奇花异卉、假山怪石，形成浓厚的庭园氛围，与园林区的风格融为一体。

宫廷区的后面，是以万寿山和昆明湖为主体的广大园林区。由于万寿山山脊南北地貌的差异，又自然形成了两个不同景观特色的景区——开朗的前山前湖景区和幽静的后山后湖景区。

　　前山前湖景区包括万寿山南坡和昆明湖。建筑师们运用突出重点、烘云托月的手法，在万寿山南坡的中央部位建置了一组体量大、形象丰富的中央建筑群——排云殿群落和佛香阁。整个前山的建筑布局以它们为中心展开，华丽的殿堂台阁，密密层层地把山坡覆盖，构成一条贯穿前山上下的中轴线，在其两侧又有对称配置的建筑群作为两翼的陪衬；尤其是佛香阁，耸立于高台之上，气宇轩昂，从而成为总揽前山乃至整个景区的构图中心。

　　园中的长廊是前山和中轴线横向联络的纽带，这一纵一横构成了前山建筑布局的纲领。其他体量较小的建筑物和建筑群，则自由而疏朗地点缀于山脚、山坡或山脊上，以此来烘托中央建筑群的浓密、端庄、华丽。整个前山重点突出，脉络清晰，主宾分明，寓变化于严整，于严整中有变化。这既体现了帝王苑囿雍容磅礴的气势，又不失园林婉约清丽的风姿。

　　昆明湖的迷人之处在于水。早在清漪园建园之初，人们在向西拓展水面时，同时修造了西堤。它纵贯昆明湖，并以支堤将湖面分割为三个大小不等的水域，每个水域有一中心岛屿，三岛屿成鼎足布局。这种"一池三山"的理水方式，是中国历代皇家园林建筑的传统内容。

　　昆明湖内最大的岛屿是南湖岛，岛北端的涵虚堂雄居于临湖的高台上，正好与湖对岸的佛香阁遥相呼应，构成对景。其次，南湖岛与东堤的十七孔桥相连，并通过长桥、廓如亭、文昌阁等建筑的过渡，与景区的构图中心佛香阁在气势上联贯起来。如果从湖的最南端绣漪桥北望，但见碧波荡漾的湖面上有南湖岛和十七孔桥障隔，在万寿山远景的衬托下，尤显得湖面深远、宽广。

　　后山后湖景区不像前山前湖景区那样开阔，这里以近观小品为主，远眺为辅，着意创造一个幽静深邃、富于山林野趣的环境。除"四大部洲"寺庙群外，大部分是自成一体的小园林，或沿山、或倚坡、或临水，结合地貌，错落设置。

　　所谓后湖，就是沿万寿山北麓开凿的一条小河，全长千余米。由于地势局促，人们利用峡口、石矶把河道障隔成六个段落，其水面的形状各异，自然形成一串具有各种景观特色的小湖面。游人泛舟湖上，或沿河岸散步，大有山重水复、柳岸花明之趣。

　　颐和园是国家重点文物保护单位，并被列入世界文化遗产名录。早在上个世纪的六十年代初，国家对破旧的颐和园进行了大规模的整修，并在园内广植花草树木，初步改变了昔日荒芜的景象。以后又对长廊进行了多次维修和油饰。八十年代以来，国家拨巨款先后对后山的"四大部洲"、前山的主体建筑佛香阁和德和园大戏楼进行全面的整修。重建了诸如苏州街、景明楼、澹宁堂等多处景观。1991年，北京市18万人参加了昆明湖的清淤工程，使成湖240多年的淤泥得到彻底清理。现在的颐和园更加美丽，更加迷人。

About the Summer Palace

The Summer Palace, in the northwestern suburbs of Beijing, about 15 kilometres away from the centre of the city, is the largest extant imperial garden in China, covering an area of over 290 hectares, about 220 hectares of which are covered by a lake. It has more than 3,000 bays of buildings including halls, towers, terraces and waterside pavilions. A complex of halls and gardens, the Summer Palace was a major place for the emperor and empress to have political activities and rest in the late period of the Qing Dynasty (1644-1911).

The Summer Palace, originally called the Garden of Clear Ripples, is formed mainly by the Longevity Hill and Kunming Lake. The Longevity Hill, an offshoot of the Yanshan Mountain Range, is about sixty metres high. At the beginning of the 12th century, the Jin Dynasty began to build a temporary palace here, channelling water from the Jade Fountain Hill to the foot of the Longevity Hill.

From the 16th century to the middle of the 19th century, Chinese gardening saw an unprecedented development, and in the middle of the 18th century, the building of imperial gardens reached a high peak. In the sixty years Emperor Qianlong reigned (1736-95), five large gardens were built in the northwestern suburbs of the capital city under Qianlcng's personal guidance. They were known as the "Three Hills and Five Gardens", namely, Garden of Everlasting Spring, Garden of Perfection and Brightness, Garden of Tranquillity and Pleasure at the Fragrant Hill, Garden of Tranquillity and Brightness at the Jade Fountain Hill and the Garden of Clear Ripples at the Longevity Hill (the predecessor of the Summer Palace).

In 1750 Emperor Qianlong, to celebrate the sixtieth birthday of his mother Empress Xiaosheng, ordered the Garden of Clear Ripples to be built. The whole project took 15 years. The newly-built garden was approximately the size of the present-day Summer Palace. At that time, the northwestern outskirts of Beijing was the site of pleasure grounds and gardens, where pavilions and lodges were nestled in the lush green woods as far as the eye could see. Emperor Qianlong, a true lover of gardens, made six trips south of the Yangtze in his lifetime and, wherever he saw a scenic spot or garden, he ordered the court painters to do sketches of the place to be used as reference materials for the construction of gardens in the north. So, incorporating southern ideas and skill without giving up northern traditions, the imperial gardens built later had both the grandeur of the north and the grace and refinement of the south.

However, during the Second Opium War, the Anglo-French Allied Forces invaded Beijing and reduced the Three Hills and Five Gardens to ashes in 1860. The seventh Qing emperor Xianfeng (reigned 1851-61) fled with his wife and concubines to Rehe (present-day Chengde) and died there the next year. After his death, Empress Dowager Cixi came into power and thus began the period known as "the rule behind the curtain", which lasted for 48 years. For several times, she urged her trusted followers to petition the emperor to restore the Garden of Clear Ripples, the Garden of Perfection and Brightness and other gardens, and had to give up because of the strong resistance of the members of the imperial house and high officials. In 1875 Emperor Guangxu succeeded to the throne. His father, Prince Yihuan, who was in charge of the Office of the Navy, wanted to curry favour with Cixi and used the navy's funds to restore the Garden of Clear Ripples under the pretext of setting up a naval academy there. The restoration was done secretly. It was not announced to the public until 1888 when the project was about to be completed. Cixi made the announcement by issuing an imperial edict in the name of the emperor and changed the garden's name to the Summer Palace.

In 1900 the Eight-Power Allied Forces invaded Beijing, Cixi fled to Xi'an, the Summer Palace was devastated a second time. The invaders took away everything valuable and destroyed the buildings. Upon her return to Beijing in 1902, Cixi ordered the garden rebuilt immediately. After the rebuilding was completed, she spent the greater part of the year here from February until November when she returned to the Forbidden City.

The Summer Palace has a special layout in construction. Because Empress Dowager Cixi needed to give audience to her ministers and hold court sessions here, a special precinct was established for this purpose,which is known as the Palace Area. However, as a component part of garden architecture, the palace halls were built somewhat differently from those in the Forbidden City. Instead of the resplendent yellow glazed tiles, the roofs of the buildings were covered with plain bluish grey tiles and, in harmony with the landscape, the courtyards were embellished with evergreens, rocks and flower beds.

The vast garden area beyond the audience halls includes the Longevity Hill and Kunming Lake. As the hill's topographical features are different, the garden area has two distinctly different kinds of scenery: the spacious open Front Hill and Front Lake Area and the quiet Back Hill and Back Lake Area.

The Front Hill and Front Lake Area is formed by the southern slope of the Longevity Hill and Kunming Lake. Here the architects resorted to the method of giving prominence to one or several main buildings. This they did by building an impressive architectural complex at the centre of the Front Hill, from which the other buildings radiated. The two main buildings in this complex are the Hall of Dispelling the Clouds and the Tower of the Fragrance of Buddha.

The Long Promenade is a link to connect the Front Hill and the central axis. It runs from east to west along the foot of the hill and is bisected by the axis and together with the latter forms the central line of the whole architectural layout in the Front Hill area. The smaller buildings and minor architectural groups in this area are scattered freely and sparsely, which has the effect of enhancing by contrast the solemnity, grandeur and compactness of the central complex. Such a layout manifests the grandeur of an imperial palace while retaining the elegance of a pleasure garden.

The charm of Kunming Lake lies on the vast expanse of the water. In the early days when the Garden of Clear Ripples was constructed, the lake was expanded westward and the West Dike was built. The dike expanded through the lake and branched out to break the lake in three, each with a small island in the centre. This was the "one pool, three hills" pattern in the tradition of imperial garden building.

South Lake Island is the largest island on Kunming Lake. At the northern end of the island stands the Hall of Forbearance and Humbleness on a high platform overlooking the lake and facing the Tower of the Fragrance of Buddha across the water. South Lake Island is linked to the East Dike by the Seventeen-Arch Bridge, and then through the bridge, the Spacious Pavilion, the Studio of Literary Prosperity and other buildings. Together with the Tower of the Fragrance of Buddha across water, grandeur is thus created. If one looks northward across the water from the Bridge of Embroidered Ripples at the southernmost tip of the lake, the Seventeen-Arch Bridge and the South Lake Island are interposed like a screen in front of the Longevity Hill, and the lake seems even vaster.

Compared with the Front Hill and Front Lake Area, the Back Hill and Back Lake Area is a narrower strip of land. It is a place mainly for enjoying the natural beauty of the woods and hills. Except for the group of lamaseries on the slope, the buildings here are sparsely laid out, most of them in small gardens on the slope or at the foot of the hill, or near the water.

The so-called Back Lake is actually a long watercourse of about 1,000 meters excavated along the northern foot of the Longevity Hill. As the water runs parallel to the natural slope on the southern side of the hill, the scene here is of a clear stream flowing through a wooded land. A number of offshore stone structures are erected at various places to break the watercourse, dividing the stream into six sections, each having a different shape and forming a small lake with distinctive natural settings.

The Summer Palace is an important historical site under state protection and has been placed on UNESCO's World Heritage list. As early as the 1950s, the state began to renovate the broken buildings and plant trees and flowers in the garden, so its old face of desolation was preliminarily changed. Later, large-scale renovations and repainting were made to the Long Promenade. After the 1980s the state allocated a large amount of funds to rebuild the massive temples, the Four Great Regions, on the slope of the back hill, and repair the complex of buildings, the Tower of the Fragrance of Buddha and the Great Stage on the front hill. The famous Suzhou Street, Jingming Hall, Danning Hall and many other buildings were rebuilt. In 1990 the Beijing Municipal Government organized 180,000 people to clear away the sludge from the bed of Kunming Lake. This was the first big thorough clean-up in 240 years. Today, the Summer Palace has become more beautiful, shining with ever greater splendour.

宫 廷 区

The Palace Area

　　进入颐和园东宫门，前行不远，即到宫廷区的正殿仁寿殿庭院，此殿两侧以配殿、内外朝房、值房共三进院落构成一组严整的建筑群。

　　中国近代史上发生的一些重大事件，如变法维新运动的发端与流产，镇压义和团运动的敕令和诏书，诸多丧权辱国条约的酝酿和签订，都是在这庞大的宫廷区里炮制、厘定和批准的。清末实际上的最高统治者慈禧太后晚年的大部分时间也是在这里度过的。光绪皇帝在这里断断续续被囚禁了近10年。这些无疑给宫廷区蒙上了一层神密的色彩。

　　人们来到宫廷区，不仅可以看到华丽的建筑，精美的装饰，奢侈的陈设，还可以了解许多帝、后生活的轶闻和趣事。

　　After entering the East Palace Gate, visitors are in the Palace Area, a group of buildings consisting of the Hall of Benevolence and Longevity and the side halls and courtyards. This group of buildings are cleverly laid out and exquisitely constructed.

　　These buildings are closely connected with some major events in modern Chinese history. It was here that the Constitutional Reform and Modernization plan rose and fell, and it was also here that the imperial decrees and edicts were issued to suppress the Yihetuan Movement. Many treaties of national betrayal and humiliation were produced here. Empress Dowager Cixi, the manipulator at the end of the Qing Dynasty, spent most of her later years here, and Emperor Guangxu was imprisoned here for nearly ten years. All this added a layer of mystery to this small palace area.

　　From here visitors can see the magnificent buildings, beautiful decorations and luxuriant furnishings of the palace and hear many anecdotes and stories about the emperor and empress.

牌楼 为颐和园首座标志性建筑，它体量宏大，三门七顶，木制结构，其上遍绘金龙"和玺"彩画。这种彩画的色调以金、红、青、绿相间，图案以龙凤为主。牌楼正面书"涵虚"二字，提示烟波浩渺；背面写"罨秀"二字，意指园林清幽。

The Archway. The first structure of the Summer Palace, this huge archway with three passages and seven roofs is constructed of wood and gorgeously painted. On its front side are the characters "Han Xu", which imply the vast expanse of water, and on the back side "Yan Xiu", which suggest the tranquillity of the park just behind it.

雕石阶 置于东宫门前，门楣悬"颐和园"匾额，为光绪皇帝手笔。石阶上为双龙戏珠浮雕，它是皇家尊严的象征，又是谕旨和敕令的标志。

Carved Stone Stairs. The stone stairs are in front of the East Palace Gate. The Horizontal Inscribed Board bears the three Chinese characters "Yi He Yuan" written in Emperor Guangxu's handwriting. The two dragons playing with a pearl carved in relief on the stone slab symbolize the dignity of the imperial family.

东宫门 是颐和园正门。门为三明两暗的庑殿式建筑。中门专供帝、后出入，称"御路"，其两侧门洞供王公大臣出入；太监、兵卒从南北两侧的边门出入。

East Palace Gate. The front entrance to the Summer Palace is a palatial building. The gate in the middle, called "The Imperial Gateway", was for the emperor and empress, the gates on either side were for princes and high officials, and the northern and southern side doors were for eunuchs and guards.

铜狮　东宫门前两侧各有一只铜狮。中国古人造狮，有较完备的传统体制，凡雄狮大多右足踏绣球，象征权力和一统天下；雌狮左足抚幼狮，象征子嗣昌盛。

Bronze Lions. On either side of the East Palace Gate stand two bronze lions: a male one and a female one. The male lion has a ball under its right paw, which is symbolic of power and unity, whereas the female lion fondles young lion with ito left paw, symbolic of prosperity of its posperity. means that "the old is always with the young".

仁寿门　为宫廷区的二重门。它巧妙地把牌楼、衙署仪门和祠庙棂星门的形式特点结合在一起，于典丽中透出庄重，是颐和园最具特色的门。

Gate of Benevolence and Longevity. This is the second gate of the Palace Area. Its combination of different styles gives a sense of solemn elegance.

仁寿殿　原名勤政殿，意为不忘勤理政务；光绪年间改为今名，意为施仁政者长寿。此殿是光绪皇帝和慈禧太后在园期间听政的大殿。

Hall of Benevolence and Longevity. Formerly called the Hall of Diligent Government, the hall was changed to its present name during the reign of Emperor Guangxu. This was where Empress Dowager Cixi and Emperor Guangxu held court and administered state affairs.

仁寿殿内景　其陈设如当年帝、后临朝状。正中高台为地平床，上设屏风、宝座、御案，两侧为珐琅塔、仙鹤和狻熏炉等。这里是中国近代史上变法维新运动策划地之一。1898年光绪皇帝曾在此召见改良派领袖康有为，揭开了维新变法的序幕。可惜好景不过百日，由于封建保守势力的镇压，光绪皇帝因此被囚10年。

Interior view of the Hall of Benevolence and Longevity. In the centre are the dais, throne and imperial table. Around it are screens, fans, crane-shaped lanterns and enameled tripods for incense and candles. This was also one of the places where the Constitutional Reform and Modernization plan was hatched. In 1898, Emperor Guangxu met Kang Youwei, leader of the reformers, and appointed him reform counselor, declaring an institutional reform. But due to the opposition of conservative forces, the reform was aborted soon, and Emperor Guangxu was imprisoned for ten years.

延年井　位于仁寿殿北，水味清甜。慈禧太后曾用此水服药解暑，特赐名"延年井"。

Long Life Well. Located to the north of the Hall of Benevolence and Longevity, the well had sweet water, with which Empress Dowager Cixi took medicine in the summer time. So she named it "Long Life Well".

玉澜堂　光绪皇帝寝宫，是一处临水而建的四合院。正殿为玉澜堂，为光绪皇帝处理日常政务的处所。

Hall of Jade Billows. This courtyard built along the bank of the lake was Emperor Guangxu's private living quarters. The main hall, the Hall of Jade Billows, was where the emperor administered state affairs.

玉澜堂内景 1898年9月16日，光绪皇帝曾在此召见握有兵权的袁世凯，令其助行新政。袁阳奉阴违，转而告密。五天后慈禧太后发布"上谕"，谎称皇帝有病，她要再次"训政"。从此皇帝被囚于玉澜堂内。为防其逃遁，东、西、北通道均被堵死，且有慈禧太后亲信日夜监视。

Interior view of the Hall of Jade Billows. On September 16, 1898, Emperor Guangxu called in Yuan Shikai, an army commander, here and instructed him to help the reformers. But Yuan Shikai quickly informed against the reformers. Five days later Empress Dowager Cixi staged a coup and placed Emperor Guangxu, who had backed the reform, under "palace arrest". To prevent the Emperor from escaping, exits to the east, west and north of the chamber were all blocked with bricks, and specially appointed eunuchs kept a round-the-clock watch on him.

藕香榭 为玉澜堂的西配殿，光绪皇帝寝宫。原为前后门的穿堂殿，出后门可观昆明湖景。慈禧太后"训政"后，后门和通道被堵。

Pavilion of Lotus Fragrance. This is the western side-building in the Hall of Jade Billows. It was originally a through building with front and back entrances and led to a pier on the lake. Later, it was blocked off after the Emperor was under house arrest here.

寝宫内景 炕上卧具为原物。光绪皇帝在这里断断续续地被囚10年，1908年11月14日病逝，年仅38岁。次日慈禧太后亦病死。

The Inside of the Pavilion. This was Emperor Guangxu's bedroom. The bed, canopy, pillow and quilts are the original ones used by the Emperor who was imprisoned here intermittently for ten years. He died of illness on November 14, 1908 at the age of 38, and a day later Empress Dowager Cixi also breathed her last.

跨院 原为玉澜堂后的第二进院落，也是连接皇帝和皇后寝宫的过渡庭院，自玉澜堂后墙被堵死后，皇帝即与此院无缘。

The Courtyard. This is the second courtyard at the back of the Hall of Jade Billows, connecting the bedroom chamber of the emperor and that of the empress. After the Hall of Jade Billows was blocked off, the emperor could not come to the courtyard any more.

夕佳楼 是跨院西侧的观景楼。

Pavilion of Beautiful Sunset. This is the pavilion to view the scenery, located on the western side of the Courtyard.

夕佳楼观景　　登上楼台，视野开阔，远看西山，近观楼阁，景色如画，美不胜收。

View from the Pavilion of Beautiful Sunset.　　When one ascends the pavilion, the distant West Hills, the pagoda, the tower and the lake, all come into view.

宜芸馆　是光绪皇帝的皇后隆裕的寝宫。隆裕姓叶赫那拉，是慈禧太后的侄女。慈禧太后选她为皇后，意在控制光绪皇帝。

Lodge of the Propriety of Weeding. The main hall in this courtyard was the bedroom of Empress Longyu. Longyu was Empress Dowager Cixi's niece. Cixi made her the empress with the purpose to control Emperor Guangxu.

乐寿堂　为一大型四合院，慈禧太后寝宫。大殿红柱灰顶，垂脊卷棚歇山式，造型别致，富丽堂皇。

Hall of Happiness in Longevity.　This large complex was Empress Dowager Cixi's residential quarters. With red pillars and a grey roof, this magnificent hall was built in a unique style.

水木自亲　位于昆明湖北岸，前轩临水，为慈禧太后的寝宫乐寿堂的正门。她由水路入园时，在这里下船直入乐寿堂大院。

Hall of Affinity Between Wood and Water.　Located on the northern bank of Kunming Lake, it is the front entrance of the Hall of Happiness in Longevity. When the Empress Dowager came to the Summer Palace by water, her boat docked here.

乐寿堂内景 其陈设十分华丽，正中设有宝座、御案、掌扇和围屏。宝座四周放着四只镀金檀香炉，其左右放置的两只青花大瓷盘，是专为慈禧太后盛水果闻香味的；殿顶还悬挂着五彩玻璃吊灯，装于1903年，这恐怕是中国最早的电灯了。

Interior view of the Hall of Happiness in Longevity. In the centre are the throne and imperial desk, surrounded by ornamental fans and screens. On the four sides are incense burners shaped like a peach. On either side of the throne is a large ceramic dish with blue floral designs. The chandeliers hung in the hall were set in 1903 and probably were the first electric lamps in China.

慈禧太后卧室　靠北墙的大床和床上黄云缎幔帐，以及其他床上用品均为原物；慈禧太后驻园期间，均在此下榻。

Empress Dowager Cixi's bedroom.　The large bed near the northern wall, the canopy and the bedding are the originals. When Empress Dowager Cixi came to the Summer Palace, she lived here.

紫玉兰 乐寿堂的玉兰多从中国南方移栽，100多年前，这里玉兰成林，有"玉香海"的美称。1860年英法联军一把火烧毁了玉兰林，现仅存一白一紫两棵树龄200多年的玉兰树。

Purple yulan. Most of the yulan magnolia behind the Hall of Happiness in Longevity were transplanted from south China. More than 100 years ago, there was a forest of yulan here known as "The Sea of Yulan Fragrance". In 1860 the Anglo-French Allied Forces burned it down. The extant two yulan, one white and the other purple, are more than 200 years old.

青芝岫 置于乐寿堂庭院，是明代太仆米万锤的遗物，后被乾隆皇帝发现，命人置于此处，取名青芝岫。巨石两边分别刻乾隆皇帝题写的"玉英"、"香莲"四字。

Blue Iris Hill. This huge boulder was abandoned by the Ming-Dynasty official Mi Wanzhong and was later found by Emperor Qianlong who ordered it brought here and gave it its name. On either side of the boulder are carved with the words "Yuying" and "Xianglian" to show the emperor's fondness.

汽车 是袁世凯送给慈禧太后的礼品。这是中国引进的第一辆汽车。

Car. This car was a present given to Empress Dowager Cixi by Yuan Shikai. This was the first imported car in China.

人力车 为日本国所赠，慈禧太后专用。车把顶端镶有铜龙，车衬和坐垫用黄软缎制作，并用金线绣有多种图案。清廷规定，一品大臣乘蓝轿，宫内大员乘红、绿轿；只有帝、后才可乘黄轿、坐黄车。

Ricksha. This ricksha was given by Japan to the Empress Dowager. On the top of the two shafts are bronze dragons, and on the cushion and lining made of silk are embroidered with various designs in gold thread. It is said that the Qing court stipulated that the top officials took blue rickshas, palace officials had red or green rickshas, only the emperor and empress used yellow ones.

永寿斋　这里是慈禧太后的心腹太监李莲英的住所。李是清末权倾朝野的大宦官，其住所装饰与陈设十分华贵。图为永寿斋正门。

Hall of Longevity. This was the living quarters of Li Lianying, the trusted eunuch of Empress Dowager Cixi. The building is most magnificent. In the picture is the front of the Hall of Longevity.

永寿斋内景　据资料记载，李莲英的卧室内挂黄软缎帘，铺黄软缎褥，几与帝王无异。

Interior view of the Hall of Longevity. The hall was also lavishly furnished. According to records, Li Lianying's beddings were made of yellow silk, which were almost the same as the emperor's.

扬仁风　　位于乐寿堂西侧，自成一院。院内最著名的建筑是"扇面殿"，殿前地面用汉白玉石拼成扇骨形；凹进的扇面墙恰似汉字"风"的"几"旁。建筑之巧，令人称奇。

Wind of Virtue. This is a courtyard northwest of the Hall of Happiness in Longevity, forming an adjunct to the latter. The most attractive building in the courtyard is the Fan Hall, before which the terrace was paved with white marble slabs radiating out like the ribs of a fan. The architecture is magnificent.

德和园　位于仁寿殿北，其主要建筑为大戏楼、颐乐殿和庆善堂。图为德和园大门。

Garden of Virtue and Harmony.　Lying northwest of the Hall of Benevolence and Longevity of Weeding, the garden consists of the Great Stage, the Hall of Health and Happiness, and Qingshan Hall. In the picture is the gate of the Garden of Virtue and Harmony.

大戏楼 建成于1895年，它与故宫的畅音阁和承德避暑山庄的清音阁，同称清代三大戏楼，但以它为最。

Great Stage. The construction of this stage was completed in 1895. This stage and the other two – the Studio of Unimpeded Sound in the Forbidden City and the Studio of Clear Sounds in the Summer Villa at Chengde in Hebei – are known as the three great stages of the Qing Dynasty. But this one is the largest of the three.

下层戏台 　大戏楼高21米，分上、中、下三层。下层戏台宽17米，天花板中心有天井与上层戏台串通，二层戏台设有绞车，可巧设机关布景，上天入地，变幻无穷。戏台底部还有一眼深井和五方水池，作为表演时所需的水源。

The stage on the lowest floor.　The Great Stage is a three-storeyed structure, 21 metres high and 17 metres wide on the lowest floor. There are chambers above and below it, with trapdoors for "angels" to descend from the "sky" and "devils" to rise up from the "earth". There is also a deep well and five square pools under the stage for water scenes.

颐乐殿　坐北朝南，与大戏楼相对，距离不足20米。这是一座专供慈禧太后看戏的殿堂，其正中设有宝座。

Hall of Health and Happiness. Facing south, this hall stands opposite to the stage in a distance of less than 20 metres. This was the place where Empress Dowager Cixi enjoyed theatrical performances.

宝座 座后设有五折屏风，宝座和屏风均为红木制作，金漆满涂，上贴浮雕的珐琅百鸟朝凤。这是慈禧太后70岁生日制作的，至今璀璨如新。

The throne. In the centre of the hall stands this gold lacquered throne with a design of a hundred birds paying homage to the phoenix. It was specially made for Cixi's seventieth birthday. It looks still new and dazzling today.

慈禧太后蜡像 据故老相传，慈禧太后看戏并不一定坐宝座，有时坐在正殿东西两侧间的炕床上隔窗观看（如图）。光绪皇帝则坐在殿外廊檐下东窗台处，而王公大臣们则按事先排定的次序，分坐在颐乐殿两侧的看戏廊里。

Waxwork of the Empress Dowager. It was said the Empress Dowager sometimes didn't sit in the throne to watch the performances but sat in bed in the wing halls to watch from the window (see the picture). Emperor Guangxu sat out on the front porch to the left of the entrance, while princes, dukes, ministers and other high officials sat along the east and west verandas on the sides.

庆善堂　在颐乐殿北还有一重院落，院内面阔五间的正殿叫庆善堂，其左右各有一座配殿。庆善堂是慈禧太后看戏时临时休息的殿堂。殿的西暖阁曾作过画室，有一幅"传神秋毫"的肖像最为她喜欢，曾被送往美国展出，至今仍在美国华盛顿博物馆。

Qingshan Hall.　On the north of the Hall of Health and Happiness there is a compound, the main hall of which is called Qingshan Hall, the resting place of Cixi when she came to watch performances. The west side-chamber was once used as a studio. There was a gorgeous portrait Cixi liked best. She ordered it sent to the United States as an entry to an art contest. Now the portrait is still housed in the Washington Museum.

西暖阁画室 端坐者为慈禧太后模拟蜡像。

The west side-chamber studio. Sitting in the chair is Empress Dowager Cixi(waxwork).

慈禧太后龙衣 用金丝线在衣上绣满龙、凤、云和寿字图案，极华贵。据说，慈禧太后仅存放在颐和园的服饰和珍宝、古玩竟有3000多箱，其中一幅披肩是用3500颗"大如黄鸟之卵"的珍珠编织而成的，由此可见其生活之奢靡。

Empress Dowager Cixi's clothes. This robe was embroidered with the pattern of dragon, phoenix and cloud in gold thread. It was said Cixi had more than 3,000 trunks of clothes, jewelry and rare curios in the Summer Palace. One of her shawls was made of 3,500 pearls, each the size of a bird egg.

▶

慈禧太后画像 1905年，荷兰画家华士·胡博（Hubert VOS）应聘为慈禧太后画像，其时她已年届七旬，但画像却显得年轻，显然是画家为讨其欢心而有意画的。

Portrait of Empress Dowager Cixi. In 1905, in her seventies, Empress Dowager Cixi asked the Dutch artist Hubert VOS to do a portrait of her. The artist painted her as a young woman in order to flatter her.

前山前湖景区

The Southern Slope and Lake Area

此景区约占全园面积的百分之九十，前山即万寿山南坡，前湖即昆明湖。山屏列于北，湖横陈于南，成北实南虚之势。

万寿山前山景区由长廊、排云殿、佛香阁以及分列于它们两侧的主要点景建筑和重点建筑物构成；昆明湖景区由南湖岛、东、西堤和堤、岛上的点景建筑构成。

在这个景区内，造园匠师们巧妙地利用建筑布局与前山的山形特点相结合，与湖中岛、堤的安排相结合，与园外"借景"的收摄相结合，来组织、点染、剪裁那些人造景观和天然风景，达到了"虽由人造，宛自天成"的艺术效果。极目所望，景区内充满诗情画意，给人以无限美感。

This scenic area includes the southern slope of Longevity Hill and Kunming Lake, taking about ninety percent of the total area of the Summer Palace. The southern slope has the Long Promenade, the Hall of Dispelling the Clouds, the Tower of the Fragrance of Buddha, and the towers and halls on both sides, while the lake area is formed by the East Dike, the West Dike, the South Lake Island and the buildings on them.

In an ingenious way the architects adapted the buildings to blend with or accentuate the natural surroundings, making them a harmonious whole. The vast expanse of Kunming Lake is embellished with an island, a long causeway and several exquisitely built bridges, and on the island are various buildings. The natural beauty is set off by a multitude of highly decorative halls, towers, galleries, pavilions and bridges; it is a poetic picture.

长廊　　中国的廊建筑源远流长。它是组织园林景观、分割园林空间、联络点景建筑和建筑群的一种带屋顶的走廊，其形式多种多样，最常见的是两面透空的游廊。中国的廊建筑最大、最长、最负盛名的就是颐和园长廊。

The Long Promenade. The building of promenade has a long history in China. A promenade is a long covered corridor, which is used to accentuate a scenic spot, to separate different scenes, or to connect buildings in a garden. They vary in style and shape. The most popular one is open to both sides. The promenade in the Summer Palace is the biggest and most famous of its kind in China.

邀月门　长廊东起邀月门，西止石丈亭，中以排云门分为东西两段，每段各伸出一截短廊连接对鸥舫和鱼藻轩两座临水建筑，全长750多米，273间画廊。

Gate of Inviting the Moon. The Long Promenade begins at the Gate of Inviting the Moon in the east and ends at the Ten-Foot Stone Pavilion and is divided into two symmetrical sections by the Gate of Dispelling the Clouds. Each section is connected leg a short corridor to a pavilion overlooking the lake water. The promenade is 750 metres long with 273 sectors.

寄澜亭　长廊共串连了"留佳"、"寄澜"、"秋水"、"清遥"四座八角重檐亭，分别象征春夏秋冬四季。亭不仅壮景，还起着支撑长廊的作用。

Jilan Pavilion. The Long Promenade has four large double-eaved octagonal pavilions, namely Liujia Pavilion, Jilan Pavilion, Qiushui Pavilion and Qingyao Pavilion, which symbolize the four seasons. These beautiful pavilions play the role of supporting the long promenade.

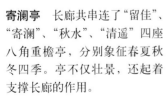

从亭内看长廊　　图为从"留佳亭"西望长廊，亭内藻井、梁枋上均布满彩画，置身其中，如在画中倘徉。

The Long Promenade viewed from the pavilion.　　In the picture is the Long Promenade viewed from Liujia Pavilion. Inside the pavilion, the caisson ceiling and beams are beautifully painted in various patterns, which make the visitors feel as if they are in an art gallery.

彩画 长廊彩画题材十分广泛，有花鸟、树石、山水、人物等。十八世纪中叶，乾隆皇帝曾派宫廷画师到杭州西湖写生，得西湖景546幅。这些湖景被悉数移绘到长廊273间画廊的梁枋上。上个世纪六十年代，中国政府不仅保留了西湖风景画，还增绘了具有民族特色的彩画14000多幅，使长廊成为名副其实的画廊。图为中国古典神话小说《西游记》中孙悟空大闹天宫的故事。

Coloured designs. The paintings in the Long Promenade cover a wide range of subjects from birds, flowers, trees, mountains, rivers and human figures. In the middle of the 18th century, Emperor Qianlong sent his court painters to do paintings of the West Lake in Hangzhou. They painted 546 different paintings and copied them on to the beams and pillars in the 273 sectors in the Long Promenade. In the 1960s, while keeping the original paintings of the West Lake, the Chinese government added 14,000 new paintings to the Long Promenade, making it a real art gallery. The painting in the picture is about the story "The Monkey King Makes Havoc in the Heavenly Palace" as described in the classical novel "Journey to the West".

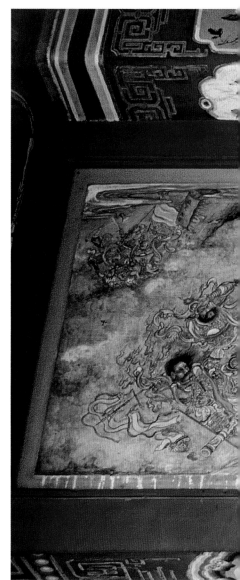

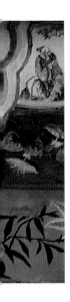

山水画 以中国传统的工笔见长，笔触工整、细腻。多数画被圈在大半圆的括线内，称为"包袱"，分布在凹凸不平的构件上，但给人的感觉却是平整而规则的。

Landscape painting. Most of the paintings in the Long Promenade are traditional pieces in meticulous brushwork. Painted in a semi-circle, they give a strong three-dimensional effect.

鱼藻轩 位于长廊西段。名为轩实为榭，面湖而立，这里有鱼有藻，名副其实。

Yuzao Pavilion. In the west section of the Long Promenade, the Yuzao Pavilion (Pavilion with Fish and Algae) faces the lake. There are really fish and algae here.

长廊观景　从邀月门西行，向南可观湖景，向北可览山色。无论阴晴雨雪，均可在长廊内游憩赏景。图为从鱼藻轩西眺。

A view from the Long Promenade. Starting from the Gate of Inviting the Moon, visitors may, rain or shine, walk westward along the promenade enjoying the scenery of the lake and the hill on the southern and northern sides.

山色湖光共一楼　　西段长廊向北伸出一短廊连接此楼，
登楼四望，山水尽览，故得此名。

The pavilion converging the scenes of the hill and the lake.
This pavilion is connected with the west section of the Long
Promenade. When one ascends it and looks afar, the hill and
the lake come into view.

石丈亭 实非亭而是殿，殿后有院，院内有一石峰高丈余，故名石丈亭。这里是长廊的西止点。

Ten-Foot Stone Pavilion. This pavilion is named after the huge stone inside its courtyard. It is the west end of the Long Promenade.

万寿山中心建筑群 是以佛香阁为中心的庞大建筑群，倚山而建，步步递高，构成一条贯穿前山上下的中轴线，这里是总揽颐和园景区的中心。

The massive buildings on the southern slope of the Longevity Hill. This impressive group of buildings are arrayed on the slope one after the other along an axis from the hill's foot to its top. Here is the central area to view the Summer Palace.

牌楼 滨湖而立。牌楼正、背两面分别写有"云辉玉宇"、"星拱瑶枢"共八字，意指这里是九天仙界，玉宇琼楼。

Decorated Archway. This large arch stands close to the lake. On its front side is inscribed "Gorgeous Clouds and Jade Eaves" and on its back side "Stars Surrounding the Jade Hub", meaning that the place is a jewelled palace in the fairyland.

排云门　是排云殿建筑群的正门。进门有两座配殿，左为"云锦"、右为"玉华"。

Gate of Dispelling the Clouds. This gate is the main entrance to the Hall of Dispelling the Clouds. Behind it are two side halls: Yunjin Hall on the left and Yuhua Hall on the right.

二宫门　门为庑殿式建筑，座落于十四级高台上，门悬"万寿无疆"匾，门前有金水池，上跨汉白玉石桥。进入此门，便是光绪皇帝为慈禧太后祝寿时行大礼的地方；百官则在门外跪拜。

The Second Palace Gate. Up a flight of 14 stone steps stands the gate with a horizontal board inscribed with "A Long, Long Life" on it. Before the gate is the Golden Water Pond with a marble bridge across it. Behind the gate is the main building, where Emperor Guangxu kowtowed to Cixi on her birthday. High officials kowtowed outside the hall.

排云殿 殿名出自东晋文学家郭璞（公元276－324年）"神仙排云出，但见金银台"的诗句。这是专门为慈禧太后过生日受贺的大殿。大殿横列复道与左右耳殿相连，共二十一间，朱柱黄瓦，金龙眩目，气势宏大。

Hall of Dispelling the Clouds. The hall was named after the poem "Excursion in Fairyland" by the Jin-Dynaty poet Guo Pu (276-324 AD): "When fairies dispel the clouds and emerge, The gold and silver terraces appear." It was built for the celebrations of Cixi's birthday. Connected with the side halls, it consists of 21 bays with red pillars and a golden tile roof.

排云殿内景　　此殿最醒目的是宝座旁有一对木雕大"寿"字，并在殿内隔扇门装饰着"卐"字不到头的花纹，寓意长寿；殿内后间分立着高过真人的"麻姑献寿"人形。大殿陈设如此奢华，但每年仅在慈禧生日时使用一次。

Interior view of the Hall of Dispelling the Clouds. In the centre of the hall stands the nine-dragon throne with a gilt lacquer screen at the back, a wood sculpture of the word "Longevity" on either side and tripods and coloured phoenixes arrayed in front. On the doors are the decorations carved in the patterns of "Longevity" to symbolize a long life. At the rear of the hall is a wood sculpture – an image of one of the legendary Eight Immortals, the gods of longevity, holding longevity peaches. The hall was lavishly furnished, but Cixi used it only once a year.

方辉殿 排云殿左有"方辉"、右有"紫霄"两座配殿，是慈禧太后生日时赐宴群臣的大殿。

Fanghui Hall. The Hall of Dispelling the Clouds has two side halls: Fanghui Hall on the left and Zixiao Hall on the right. They were the place Cixi gave banquet to high officials on her birthday.

远眺佛香阁 佛香阁建在高21米的巨石台基上，它南俯昆明湖，背靠智慧海佛殿，以它为中心的各建筑群严整而对称地向两翼展开，彼此呼应，蔚为壮观。1860年，佛香阁被英法联军烧毁，后照原样重建，是座宗教建筑。

Tower of the Fragrance of Buddha viewed from a distance. The tower was built on a 21-metre high square platform of solid stones at the centre of the southern slope of the Longevity Hill. With the Sea-of-Wisdom Temple behind its back, it faces Kunming Lake. From it other buildings fan out eastward and westward in an orderly and symmetrical fashion. The tower was destroyed by the Anglo-French Allied Forces in 1860, and was rebuilt later according to its original form.

佛香阁 高36.48米，八面三层四重檐，顶覆黄琉璃瓦绿剪边，飞檐翘角，鎏金宝顶，气势非凡。

Tower of the Fragrance of Buddha. The tower, 36.48 metres high, is a three-storeyed octagonal structure with four tiers of eaves, upturned ridges, glazed tile roof and a gold-plated top. It is a most magnificent building.

佛香阁雪霁

Tower of the Fragrance of Buddha after snow.

南无大悲观世音菩萨 供于佛香阁一层，明万历二年（公元1574年）铸造，高五米，重万斤。

Statue of Bodhisattva. Enshrined on the first floor of the Tower of the Fragrance of Buddha, the statue was cast in the second year of Wanli Reign of the Ming Dynasty (1574). Five metres high, it weighs 10,000 catties.

佛香阁三层壁画 共8幅，环贴于正中天井井壁，内容为天仙神女。三层还存放着有关佛香阁史料和部分图片，供游人阅览。

Mural paintings. These murals, eight all together, are on the walls of the third floor of the Tower of the Fragrance of Buddha, depicting fairies and goddesses. Also on the third floor are historical materials about the building of the tower and pictures about the changes of the four seasons.

《万寿山昆明湖记》拓片 碑文为乾隆皇帝手笔，概述了京城西、北郊水系变化的历史沿革。拓片镶装于佛香阁二层。

Rubbing of "Note of the Longevity Hill and Kunming Lake". This huge note in Emperor Qianlong's handwriting is inlaid on the front side on the second floor of the Tower of the Fragrance of Buddha. It records the history of the development of the river system in the northwestern suburbs of Beijing.

从佛香阁看昆明湖 从上俯视，眼前一片金黄，远处烟波浩渺、点点游船浮动，堤、岛翠色朦胧。

A view of Kunming Lake from the Tower of the Fragrance of Buddha. Viewed from the tower, the lake is a vast expanse of water dotted with small boats, dikes and green islets.

智慧海 为万寿山的制高建筑。"智慧海"语出佛经，意为如来佛智慧似海。在它的前面是众香界牌坊。两座建筑均为砖石结构，不施寸木。智慧海又称"无梁殿"，其墙面全部用五色琉璃瓦镶贴并嵌有1000多尊无量寿佛。殿内供有观世音菩萨坐像。

Sea-of-Wisdom Temple. This temple at the top of the Longevity Hill built entirely of brick and stone, without a single beam or rafter, is popularly called the "beamless hall". Its plainness is relieved by green and yellow glaze on the outside. The outer walls have rows of over one thousand exquisitely carved Buddha statuettes. Inside the temple is enshrined the statue of Guanyin.

菩萨坐像 供于大殿正中。据佛教传说，此佛是南海普陀山观世音菩萨。她左手托甘露宝瓶，右手持杨柳枝，法力无边。本尊菩萨通体贴金箔，安坐在莲花宝座上，神情慈善安祥。

Statue of Guanyin. This statue is placed in the centre of the temple. According to mythology, Guanyin with a precious bottle in her right hand and a willow branch in her left hand has boundless magic power. This statue of Guanyin covered with goldleaf sits at ease on a lotus throne.

从万寿山顶眺望昆明湖

**Kunming Lake viewed from the
top of the Longevity Hill.**

五方阁 位于佛香阁西侧，在其中心汉白玉石台基上耸立着闻名遐迩的铜亭。"五方"系佛家语"五方色"的意思，"五方阁"意为聚五方之色的高阁。

Five-Square Pavilions. West of the Tower of the Fragrance of Buddha is a cluster of buildings, with galleries on all four sides and four small pavilions in the four corners. In the centre is the famous Bronze Pavilion resting on a base of carved white marble. Five-Square Pavilions means it embodies the colours from all sides, symbolizing peace and prosperity in the world.

宝云阁 俗称铜亭，内供佛像，但两次遭浩劫，佛像及亭的部分构件被偷运海外。铜亭铸造于1755年，高7.55米，重207吨。据史料记载，铸造时为磨光表面，仅锉下的铜屑就重5吨多。亭为重檐方顶，其菱花、隔扇、柱、梁、斗拱、椽、瓦以及九龙匾、对联等，都同木结构一模一样，通体成蟹青冷古铜色，其形庄重，铸造精细，堪为世界罕见的青铜建筑精品。

Pavilion of Precious Clouds. Also called the Bronze Pavilion, it had a statue of Buddha in it, but twice it met with catastrophe. The statue of Buddha and some parts of the bronze pavilion were taken abroad by foreign invaders. The Bronze Pavilion, cast in 1755, is 7.55 metres high and weighs 207 tons. According to historical record, it had a polished surface and the bronze filings amounted to five tons. The double-eaved roof, the partitions with waterchestnut designs, the beams, columns, lintels, rafters, brackets, tiles and pinnacle, the couplets and nine-dragon plaque, are exactly the same in form and design as those of a wooden pavilion, but all are of bronze and of a greenish-grey hue. It is a superb piece of architecture rarely found anywhere in the world.

转轮藏　位于佛香阁东侧，由正殿、配亭和"万寿山昆明湖"石碑组成。这里是帝、后贮藏经书、佛像和念经祈祷的地方。

Revolving Archive. This group of buildings east of the Tower of the Fragrance of Buddha consists of the main building, the side pavilions and the large stone tablet bearing the inscription "The Longevity Hill and Kunming Lake." It was the place where the emperors and empresses kept copies of Buddhist scriptures and Buddha portraits and chanted scriptures and said their prayers.

藏经亭　共两座，分别坐落正殿前两侧。亭中设有八面可藏经书和佛像的木塔，塔有中轴，推之可转动。帝、后入亭祷告，只须轻轻转动木塔，就算把经书念了一遍，所以叫"转轮藏"。

Archive towers. The octagonal wooden towers inside the two side pavilions were for storing Buddhist scriptures and Buddha portraits. They revolved around a central axis controlled by a mechanism below. When emperors and empresses came to chant scriptures and say their prayers, they just turned the towers, hence the name "Revolving Archive".

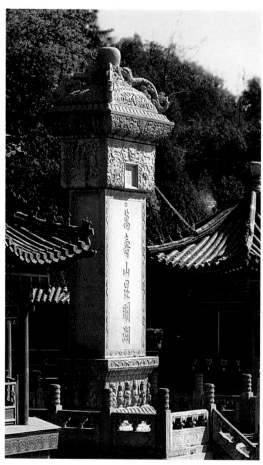

石碑 立于转轮藏正中，建于1751年。正面刻"万寿山昆明湖"六个大字，背面刻《万寿山昆明湖》碑文一篇，均为乾隆皇帝御笔。

Stone tablet. This beautifully carved tablet was erected in 1751 just at the centre of the Revolving Archive. On its front side are the words "The Longevity Hill and Kunming Lake" and on its back side is the full text of "Note of the Longevity Hill and Kunming Lake" written in Emperor Qianlong's handwriting.

写秋轩 背山而建，左右以小廊下接"寻云"、"观生意"二亭，是一处点景建筑。乾隆年间这里遍植黄栌树，深秋红叶映轩，景色迷人。

Pavilion for Writing about Autumn. Built on the slope of the hill, this pavilion is connected with two towers through a small corridor. Smoke trees were planted around here in the Qianlong Period. In late autumn, when the tree leaves turn red, the red leaves and the pavilion form a fascinating picture.

福荫轩　俗名书券殿，半弧形三间。在它西面岩石间刻有"燕台大观"四字。由此可南望昆明湖，烟云苍溟，云水尽览。

Pavilion of Blessed Shade. Also known as Shujuan Hall, this pavilion consists of three bays. On the rock west of the pavilion is carved "Yantai Grand View". From here there is an excellent view of the misty Kunming Lake.

▶

千峰彩翠 位于万寿山东部山脊，为城关式建筑。据民间传说，1888年重建颐和园工程行将结束时，风鉴家认为山顶太空，可望见园外六郎庄，而汉字"郎"、"狼"谐音，慈禧太后属相为羊，一羊遇一狼尚且不敌，何况如今一羊遇六狼，所以内忧外患频仍。于是建议修这座城关式建筑以镇六狼，并把六郎庄改名太平庄。

Thousand Green Peaks Tower. Located on the eastern top of the hill, this tower is in the style of a city gate. According to a folktale, when the rebuilding of the Summer Palace was about to complete, the geomancer found that there were little buildings on the top of the hill, from where Liulang Village outside the park could be seen. "Liulang" is the homophony of "six wolves" in Chinese. The geomancer thought: as the Empress Dowager was born in the year of sheep, how can a sheep stand against six wolves? This probably is the reason why the country is besieged with domestic trouble and foreign invasion. So he suggested that the tower be built here and changed the name of the village from "Liulang Village" to "Pacific Village".

紫气东来 位于万寿山东南半坡，为双层四角飞檐关楼。"紫气"多指祥瑞之气。清晨至此，旭日初升，晨雾升腾，确有瑞气绕身之感。图为城关北门洞。

Tower of Violet Clouds Coming from the East. This is a two-storeyed building with double-eaved roof on the eastern slope of the Longevity Hill. Violet clouds mean auspicious clouds. In early morning at sunrise, the tower is covered in mist as if everything is surrounded by violet clouds.

荟亭　为两个六角亭套合而成，因坐落于山脊，既为点景，又是观景亭。

Pavilion of Luxuriant Growth. Formed with two hexagon towers in the shape of a bat, this pavilion also provides excellent views of the landscape.

益寿堂 为一四合院，内有正堂五间，配堂两座，四周围以砖墙，墙上刻满花纹图案。1949年春3月，毛泽东主席曾在此宴请在京的民主人士。随后，在《和柳亚子先生》的诗中写下了"莫道昆明池水浅，观鱼胜过富春江"的著名诗句。

Hall of Benefit and Longevity. This is a courtyard with a main hall of five bays and two side halls. Their four walls are carved with various patterns. In March, 1949, Chairman Mao Zedong held a banquet here to entertain democratic personages, after which he wrote a poem entitled "To Mr Liu Yazi". Two lines run as follows: "Do not say that the waters of Kunming Lake are too shallow; For watching fish they are better than Fuchun River."

景福阁　前后各五间，有曲廊相通。依栏凭眺，湖光山色，美不胜收。相传，慈禧太后每年7月初7在此祭牛郎织女，8月中秋在此赏月，9月重阳在此品尝野味；盛夏常在此和后、妃、宫女们押宝、推牌九。

Pavilion of Blessed Scenery.　This pavilion, in five bays at the front and back with a surrounding corridor, commands a good view of the lake and its surrounding landscape. Empress Dowager Cixi came here to worship the Cowherd and the Girl Weaver on the seventh day of the seventh month every lunar year; enjoy the moon at the Mid-autumn Festival; eat rare game at the Double-ninth Festival; or play cards with empresses, consorts and palace maids in the summer time.

景福阁敞厅 实为抱厦。其天花板及梁枋绘满彩画。这种彩画以花鸟鱼虫为题材，以工笔精描为特色，以青、绿为底衬，人们称之为"苏式彩画"。在颐和园，除长廊彩画外，景福阁敞厅彩画是颇为精彩的。

The open hall of the Pavilion of Blessed Scenery. The hall is a pavilion with painted beams and ceilings. These paintings take flowers, birds, fish and insects as their themes and are executed in meticulous brushwork and set out with the colour of blue and green. They are called "The Su-style Painting". In addition to the paintings in the Long Promenade, the paintings here are the most beautiful in the Summer Palace.

画中游　为佛香阁西侧较大的点景建筑，共有三亭二楼一斋一牌坊。主体建筑是双层八角重檐的大敞亭。此组建筑倚山高筑，游人至此，居高临下，循廊观景，一步一趣，仿佛置身于画中，故名"画中游"。

Strolling Through A Picture. This complex of buildings stands on the hillside west of the Tower of the Fragrance of Buddha. It has three pavilions, two towers, a studio and an arched gateway. The main building is a large octagonal two-storeyed open pavilion with a double-eaved roof of green and yellow glazed tiles. When visitors come here, they find a different scene at each step they take and have the feeling of strolling through a picture.

爱山楼 画中游东有爱山楼，西有借秋楼，极似一主二仆，相伴相随。二楼后有曲廊、小径与其他建筑相通。循径登石，爬廊钻洞，其乐无穷。

Tower for Loving the Hill. To the east of the complex of buildings of Strolling Through A Picture stands the Tower for Loving the Hill and to the west is the Tower for Borrowing Autumn. Behind the two towers are meandering corridors and paths leading to other buildings. Walking along the corridors, paths , one would fend it most pleasant.

养云轩　位于万寿山东麓，门楼似钟形。额上"川泳云飞"四字为乾隆皇帝御题。门前有荷塘，形如葫芦，所以也称"葫芦河"，上架石桥。门内有轩五间，为清代妃嫔休息之所。

Clouds Gathering Pavilion. This pavilion, in the north of the eastern end of the Long Promenade, has a door in the shape of a bell. Above the door are carved the words "Winding Stream and Flying Clouds" in Emperor Qianlong's handwriting. In the front of the pavilion is a lotus pond in the shape of a gourd with a bridge across it. The five halls inside it were the resting place of imperial consorts.

听鹂馆　顶设戏台。正门匾额"金支秀华"原指古乐器上装饰的金花，这里喻宫廷艺术如金枝丽花。听鹂馆现已辟为旅游餐厅，游客可在此品尝宫廷佳肴。

Pavilion for Listening to Orioles. Inside the pavilion there is a two-storeyed stage for theatrical performances. Above the front gate of the pavilion is the inscription "Golden Branches and Beautiful Flowers". Today, the pavilion has been transformed into a large restaurant serving many of the famous dishes once prepared in the imperial kitchen.

小戏台　在德和园大戏楼建成前，慈禧太后常在此看戏。

Small stage. Empress Dowager Cixi was fond of operas. She often came here to enjoy performances before the much larger Great Stage in the Garden of Virtue and Harmony was completed.

湖山真意亭　穿过爱山楼曲径，出垂花门楼，继续上攀，即到湖山真意亭。它坐落于西部山脊，可眺望玉泉山顶的"玉峰塔"影和西山群峰。

Tower of the True Meaning of the Lake and Hill. This tower stands at the western ridge of the Longevity Hill. From here, one can see the Jade Peak Pagoda on top of the Jade Fountain Hill and the undulating west hills.

清晏舫　又名石舫，建于1755年。舫身系用巨石雕造而成。通长36米，有上下两层舱房。取意"水能载舟亦能覆舟"，喻示清王朝坚如磐石，水不能覆。

Boat of Purity and Ease. Popularly known as the Marble Boat, the boat was built in 1755. It is 36 metres long, with a hull and upper deck made of massive stone slabs. The saying goes: "Water can carry a boat, and it can also capsize a boat." By following the allusion, the marble boat was built to mean that the Qing Dynasty would be as solid as rock and never fall.

石舫底舱　舱为石木结构，地墁花砖，窗嵌五色玻璃。盛夏时慈禧太后常在舱内用早点、吃夜宵，故将石舫命名"清晏舫"。据另说，"海清河晏"为中国成语，比喻天下太平，取其为石舫名，寓意清王朝国泰民安。

The cabin of the boat. The cabin is made of wood, the lower deck is paved with floral bricks, and the windows are of stained glass with mosaic design. The old Empress Dowager often had her breakfast and dinner in the cabin in the summer time. A saying goes: the name of the marble boat came from a Chinese idiom on peace and tranquillity, which meant that the country was prosperous and the people lived in peace under the rule of the Qing court.

宿云檐　为一独立无靠的关城。城上原有楼，内供三国时代（公元220－280年）蜀汉名将关羽塑像，后改为亭式建筑，已无供像。登关南望，可见西所买卖街（小苏州街）遗址。

Tower for Gathering Clouds. This is an independent tower. Originally, inside the tower there was a statue of Guan Yu, a hero during the Three Kingdoms period (220-280 AD), but later the statue was removed. From the tower one can see the ruins of the little Suzhou Street.

荇桥　位于石舫北，横跨小苏州河。桥亭为重檐四角方形，桥墩两端有石狮；此桥体量较大，设计和建造很有特色。

Bridge of Floating Hearts. North of the Marble Boat is a stone bridge with an open pavilion above it, called the Bridge of Floating Hearts. The pavilion has a double-eaved roof and the bridge has exquisitely carved lions on its piers. The design and building are most unique in style.

西堤鸟瞰 水面上平卧一条长数里的湖堤，它就是仿风景名城杭州西湖苏堤建造的西堤。堤上除景明楼外没有其他高大建筑，但有六座造型各异的小桥点缀堤上，这里与前山浓烈的情景构成强烈的景观对比效果。

A bird's-eye view of the West Dike. At Kunming Lake there is a long causeway, the West Dike, which was built by modelling after the Su Dike in West Lake in Hangzhou. The dike has no tall buildings, except Jingming Hall. Dotted with six small bridges, it is very quiet. The tranquillity sets a striking contrast to the magnificent buildings on the front slope of the Longevity Hill.

从西堤看万寿山风景区

A view of the Longevity Hill from the West Dike.

玉带桥 拱高而薄，呈曲线形，宛若玉带。它是西堤诸桥中唯一具有实用功能的桥。桥下为昆明湖的入水口，当年帝、后走水路去玉泉山，须经此桥。

Jade Belt Bridge. The bridge is of white marble and granite, with a thin high-arched body resembling a jade belt and balustrades with carved designs of "fairy cranes" flying into the clouds. The imperial boats used to pass this point when the emperor and empress went from Kunming Lake to Jade Fountain Hill by water.

界湖桥 为西堤从北至南的首座桥，它平卧水面，造型简约，是前山通往西堤的必经之路。

Bridge by the Lake. This is the first bridge of the West Dike from north to south. Lying above water surface, this simply built bridge is a passage from the front slope of the Longevity Hill to the West Dike.

镜桥　桥名出自李白"两水夹明镜，双桥落彩虹"诗句。乾隆皇帝亦曾赋诗道："莫道湖光宛是镜，阿谁不是镜中人"。

Mirror Bridge. The bridge takes its name from two lines of a poem by the Tang poet Li Bai: "A mirror between two bodies of water; a rainbow beneath two bridges." Emperor Qianlong also wrote a poem for it with two lines running like this: "If the lake looks like a mirror, who'd be the people who don't want to be in it?"

豳风桥　桥名源于2000多年前中国第一部诗歌总集《诗经》中的"豳风"诗。豳风记录的是奴隶生产的诗歌，生活气息极浓，以此名桥，大约是想表明帝王们对庶民生活的重视。

State Song Bridge. This bridge was named after the title of a poem from the "Book of Songs", China's first collection of poetry, dating from two thousand years ago. The poem was about slave labour. The reason it was chosen for the name of the bridge was probably because the emperor wanted to show he cared about the life of the common people.

西堤古柳　西堤广植槐柳，有的柳树树龄已百年之余，每当春暖花开，花红柳绿，别有一番情趣。

Ancient willow trees on the West Dike. Willow trees are planted on the West Dike, and some of the trees are more than 100 years old. When spring comes every year, all the willow trees turn green, making the dike very beautiful.

柳桥　桥名取自"柳桥清有絮"诗句。每当春夏季节，这里花红柳绿，湖草青青，加之玉峰宝塔如画，西山翠峰似屏，别有一番诗情画意。但凡到此游览的旅客，无不为之倾倒。

Willow Bridge. The name of the bridge comes from a line of a poem: "Willow bridge is bright, covered with catkins." The dike here is lined with hanging willows, and the area of the lake is covered by green reeds. The Jade Fountain Hill and the pagoda can be seen from here, the peaks of West Hills loom like a screen in the distance, forming a poetic picture for all visitors.

景明楼 原楼建于清乾隆年间，后倾塌，上世纪九十年代修复。其名出自宋代范仲淹《岳阳楼记》"春和景明，波澜不惊"诗句的意境。主楼西侧各有一座重檐配楼，是西堤唯一高大宏阔的建筑。

Jingming Hall. This hall was first built in the Qianlong Period of the Qing Dynasty and rebuilt in the 1990s. The name of the hall was taken from a line in the essay "Yueyang Pavilion" by Fan Zhongyan of the Song Dynasty. The main hall is flanked by two side halls. It is an important sight on the western bank of Kunming Lake.

柳林 在西堤的南端，有一片以柳树为主的树林，林中小鸟啾啾，花草萋萋，彩蝶翻飞，景色十分迷人。

Willow forest. At the southern end of the West Dike is a large stretch of forest of willow trees, where birds sing and coloured butterflies dance among green grass. The scenery is very fascinating.

从东堤远眺颐和园

A view of the Summer Palace from the East Dike.

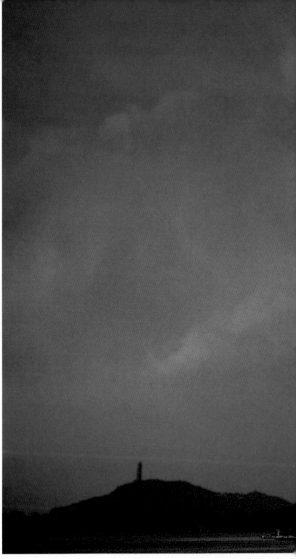

绣漪桥 位于颐和园南端，它是该园水路门户，建于清乾隆年间，但凡清宫帝、后从水路来颐和园必经此桥。由此桥右向北游览，即进入东堤风景区。

Bridge of Embroidered Ripples. Lying at the southern end of the Summer Palace as an entrance to the garden by water, the bridge was built in the Qianlong Period. The emperor and empress passed this bridge first when they came to the Summer Palace by water. From here to the north is the East Dike scenic area.

十七孔桥 　东接东堤，西连南湖岛，长150米，有如长虹卧波，蔚为壮观。

Seventeen-Arch Bridge. This bridge links the East Dike at its eastern end and connects South Lake Island at its western end. It is 150 metres long and looks like a rainbow on the lake.

石狮　桥头及桥栏望柱上共雕有544只石狮，其形态无一雷同。

Stone lions. The Seventeen-Arch Bridge has 544 stone lions on the top of balusters. Each of these stone lions has its own posture.

南湖岛俯瞰 南湖岛位于昆明湖东水域，岛上松柏森森，楼阁水榭如画，清宫太监们称它为"蓬莱岛"。其景色之美，确如东海蓬莱仙岛。

South Lake Island. Located in the eastern part of Kunming Lake, this island has ancient pines and cypresses, exquisitely built halls, pavilions and towers on it. The eunuchs of the Qing court called it the Penglai Isle as it is as beautiful as the mythical isle of Penglai, the home of immortals.

远眺涵虚堂 涵虚堂位于岛之北，石台高筑，临湖雄居，隔水与佛香阁遥相呼应。慈禧太后曾率光绪皇帝和后、妃们在此观看清海军演习水操。

Hall of Forbearance and Humbleness. This hall stands on the artificial hill of heaped rocks in the northern part of South Lake Island. It faces the Tower of the Fragrance of Buddha across the wide expanse of Kunming Lake. This is where Empress Dowager Cixi led Emperor Guangxu, the empress and consorts to watch naval exercises on the lake.

龙王塑像 中国人自古视龙为神，认为龙可呼风唤雨，能镇水害，故塑金身以祭祀。这里的龙王庙以点景为主，亦有镇水之意。

Statue of the Dragon King. Since ancient times Chinese people have regarded the dragon as god who can summon wind and rain and control water and sculptured the statue of the Dragon King for worshipping in the temple. The Dragon King's Temple here was built with the purpose to decorate the island as well as to be a symbol to subdue water.

◄

龙王庙 即广润灵雨祠，因宋代真宗皇帝（公元998－1022年在位）曾封西海龙王为广润王，昆明湖前身名西海，故取此名。龙王庙正南有一小岛名凤凰墩，其上原有凤凰楼，内置铜凤。龙、凤是帝、后的象征，北龙南凤既成对景，又有龙、凤呈祥之意。

The Dragon King's Temple. This temple is also called the Temple of Beneficial and Blessed Rain. Emperor Zhenzong (reigned 998-1022) of the Song Dynasty made the Dragon King of the West Sea the Prince of the Beneficial and Blessed Rain, and Kunming Lake was formerly called the West Sea, hence the present name of the temple. To the south of the temple is an islet called the Phoenix Mound, on which there is a pavilion with a bronze phoenix in it. The dragon and the phoenix are the symbols of the emperor and the empress. With the dragon in the south and the phoenix in the north, it gives a very auspicious meaning.

廓如亭　为八角重檐亭，面积130多平方米，由内外三层二十四根圆柱和十六根方柱支撑。亭形厚重、沉稳，气势雄浑，是中国亭建筑中最大的一座。

Spacious Pavilion. This pavilion of unusual size is octagonal and double-eaved, covering an area of 130 square metres. It has 24 round pillars and 16 square pillars, making it the biggest pavilion of its kind in China.

藻井 廓如亭藻井，层层上叠，视之眩目。藻井梁枋遍施彩画。在清代，帝、后们常在亭内饮宴，或与文人雅士们会酒赋诗。亭内悬挂的诗匾，多为乾隆皇帝诗文。

Caisson ceiling of the Spacious Pavilion. The beams and panels of the pavilion are dazzlingly painted in different colours. During the Qing Dynasty the emperor and express often held banquets here, and sometimes the emperor and his scholars would drink wine and compose poems here. Tablets with Emperor Qianlong's poems and couplets written by the scholars in response to his verses still hang in the pavilion.

铜牛 铸造于1755年。它两角耸立，双耳竖起，目光炯炯，形象逼真。牛背上铸有80字篆体铭文，说明它是用来镇水的。

Bronze ox. Cast in 1755, the ox has its head raised, its horns turned upward and its eyes fixed ahead. On its back is cast an inscription in 80 characters to explain its presence. The ox was also used as a symbol to subdue water.

文昌阁　城关式建筑，上有十字形二层楼阁，内供文昌帝君铜像。"文昌"本是星名，星相家认为此星主大贵，道教则尊它为功名利禄之神。文昌阁居昆明湖东，供文神；宿云檐位于昆明湖西，供武圣，象征文武显圣。这里妙不在寓意象征，而在建园匠师的巧妙对景。

Studio of Literary Prosperity. Standing at the northern end of the East Dike, the studio is a building in the shape of a city wall tower. Inside the two-storeyed building is enshrined the bronze statue of the God of Literary Prosperity. This building stands east of Kunming Lake with a civil god in it, while the Tower for Gathering Clouds stands west of the lake with a military god in it. It symbolizes that the two gods make their presence felt. This reflects the ingenuity of the architects in designing of the garden.

耶律楚材祠　耶律楚材是契丹族人，元代著名政治家，官至中书令（宰相）。他为维护中华民族的利益作出过重大贡献，死后根据其遗愿，安葬于燕京故里的瓮山脚下。清代保留了他的墓冢，并建祠纪念。

Yelu Chucai Temple. Yelu Chucai, a Khitan, was a famous politician of the Yuan Dynasty. During his lifetime he greatly contributed to the preservation of China's interests. After he died he was buried at the foot of Jar Hill. In the Qing Dynasty his tomb was left intact and a temple was built to commemorate him.

耶律楚材塑像　为清代塑造的彩色坐像。

Statue of Yelu Chucai. This statue was sculpted in the Qing Dynasty.

知春亭　　四面临水，亭畔点缀着山石。虽是瑞雪铺地，但冰已开始融化，柳已开始吐绿，春的信息最早来到这里，故名知春亭。

Pavilion Heralding Spring. The pavilion is surrounded by water on four sides and with many scattered rockeries around it. In early spring, when the ice begins to thaw, willows around the pavilion turn a tender green, signalling that spring has returned, hence the name of the pavilion.

后山后湖景区

The Back Hill and
Back Lake Area

景区包括万寿山北坡和一条人工开凿的后溪河，总面积约30多公顷。

后山沟壑纵横，地势起伏，水清山幽。据史料记载，乾隆年间，后山曾分别建有八处风格各异的小园式风景点。1860年英法联军入侵后，后山后湖除一座多宝琉璃塔外，所有建筑荡然无存。光绪年间重修颐和园时，因财力不足，采取拆东补西的办法，将后山有用之材挪至前山修补景点，只在香岩宗印之阁原址改建了一座佛殿。致使后山后湖在长达半个多世纪里荒芜不堪，游人不愿涉足。

自二十世纪六十年代后，中国政府花费大量人力物力，在后山植树造林，栽花种草，并重建了规模宏大的四大部洲寺庙群，恢复了具有江南水乡情趣的苏州街，使后山后湖重放异彩。

The Back Hill and Back Lake Area encompasses the northern slope of the Longevity Hill and the man-made Back Lake, covering a space of over 30 hectares. The Back Hill is an undulating slope criss-crossed by gullies and ditches. It is a very quiet place. According to historical records, there were eight gardens of different sizes built on the slope during the Qianlong Period. Unfortunately, with the exception of the Glazed Tile Pagoda of Many Treasures, all these elegant little gardens were reduced to ashes by the Anglo-French Allied Forces in 1860. When the Summer Palace was rebuilt during the Guangxu Period, because of the shortage of funds, only a Buddhist temple was constructed at the former site of the Pavilion of Fragrant Rocks and Ancestral Seals. For over a century the Back Hill and Back Lake lay waste, where no one went to visit. After the 1960s, the Chinese government began to plant trees, plants and flowers on the Back Hill. The massive temple buildings of the Four Great Regions were rebuilt and Suzhou Street, typical of the reverside street in south China, was restored.

后山后湖景区鸟瞰

A bird's-eye view of the Back Hill and Back Lake Area.

半壁桥 在颐和园西北端有两座石桥跨越后溪河，西为半壁桥，东为石桥，穿过它们，即依次进入后湖的六个小湖面，两岸桃柳掩映，临水码头和各式建筑物时隐时现，极富江南水乡情调。

Banbi Bridge. At the northwestern end of the Summer Palace there are two bridges: Banbi Bridge in the west and the Stone Bridge in the east. Behind them are the six small lakes. With peach and willow trees, piers and various buildings on the banks of the lakes, the place is much like the area in Yangtze Valley.

后湖野趣 后湖全长1000多米，乍宽乍窄，最宽处约60米，最窄外仅10米。河岸松柏苍翠，杨柳依依，野花吐艳，颇有一番乡间野趣。

Back Lake. The Back Lake is over 1,000 metres long. At some places it is 60 metres wide and at other places it is only 10 metres wide. On its two banks are tall green pines, cypresses, weeping willows and wild flowers.

谐趣园　位于后山东麓。大园林中包含小园林，是清代大型皇家园林的特征之一，被称为"园中之园"。谐趣园就是运用此种造园手法，仿江南名园——无锡寄畅园而修建的。园内有五处轩堂，七座亭榭，百间游廊，五座小桥。所有建筑环荷池展开，颇有江南园林妩媚清秀特色。

Garden of Harmonious Pleasures. On the eastern side of the Back Hill, this garden is a reproduction of a famous south China garden called Jichangyuan in Wuxi. Also known as "The Garden Within A Garden", it is typical of the large imperial gardens of the Qing Dynasty. It has five halls, seven pavilions, a hundred bays of promenades and five small bridges. All the buildings are around a lotus pond. The south China atmosphere inside the garden is palpable.

饮绿水榭　临水而建，是慈禧太后垂钓的地方。

Pavilion for Taking in the Green. Close to the pond, the pavilion was the place where Empress Dowager Cixi did fishing.

涵远堂 为谐趣园主体建筑，是慈禧太后在园期间休息的便殿。

Hall of Magnanimity. This hall is the main building in the Garden of Harmonious Pleasures, the resting place of the old Empress Dowager.

寻石迳 置于园内兰亭中，碑正面书"寻石迳"三字，背面为抒情五言诗，均为乾隆皇帝御笔。

Tablet of Looking for Stone Path. This tablet stands in a tower in the garden. On its front side are carved the words "Looking for Stone Path" and on its back side is a lyric poem. Both the inscription and the poem are in Emperor Qianlong's handwriting.

◄
半廊 中国的廊建筑形式多样，诸如两面透空的"游廊"，弯弯曲曲的"曲廊"，以墙隔为双层空间的"里外廊"，遁坡势起伏的"爬山廊"和阶梯状的"迭落廊"等等。半廊为一边透空一边有墙，墙上什锦窗造型各异，凭窗观望，一窗一景。

Half-Open Promenade. The building of promenade has a great variety of styles in China, such as "Covered Corridor", "Zigzag Gallery", "Inner and Outer Corridor", "Climbing Corridor" and "Falling Corridor". The Half-Open Promenade here has one side open and the other closed by a brick wall. In the wall are windows of different shapes from which one can see different views.

湛清轩 轩前有花圃、山石，轩左为游廊，轩右为曲径、假山。布置典雅，环境清静。

Pavilion of Profound Purity. The pavilion has a flower nursery and rockery on its front side with a winding path and rockery on its eastern side. It is very elegant and peaceful.

玉琴峡 位于谐趣园西北角。人们将山石凿成宽1至2米、长20多米的曲折的石峡，引后湖之水跌落而下，水声如琴唱，故名玉琴峡。

Jade Zither Gorge. The gorge is in the northwestern corner of the Garden of Harmonious Pleasures. The sound of water flowing in from the Back Lake is said to resemble the music of a zither.

知鱼桥　桥身贴近水面，极便观鱼。桥名源于公元前中国两位哲学家庄子和惠施的一次观鱼对话。庄子说："鱼儿出来了，鱼儿真快乐。"惠施问道："你不是鱼，怎知鱼之乐？"庄子反驳道："你不是我，怎知我不知鱼之乐？"

Know-Your-Fish Bridge. The bridge is built close to the surface of the water so as to enable people to see the fish playing in the water clearly. The bridge's name comes from an amusing dialogue between two ancient philosophers, Zhuangzi and Huizi. Zhuangzi said: "The fish is really happy." Huizi asked: "You are not a fish, how do you know fish is happy?" Zhuangzi asked back: "You are not me, how do you know I don't know the fish is happy?"

谐趣园冬景

Garden of Harmonious Pleasures in Snow.

寅辉城关 位于后山东部，突兀而立。东边石额刻"寅辉"二字，西边刻"挹爽"二字。城关左控山谷，右临后湖，关前石桥跨越山涧，俨然雄关要塞。

Tower of Early Morning Light. A representation of a city gate, the tower stands on the eastern side of the Back Hill like a sentinel guarding the slope overlooking the lake. It is across a stone bridge built over a gully, which gives the place the appearance of a mountain fortress. A stone tablet on the east wall bears the words "Early Morning Light", a similar one on the west wall is inscribed "Exuding Pleasures".

四大部洲 是乾隆年间兴建的一座藏式宗教建筑，1860年被英法联军焚毁，上世纪下半叶重建，基本恢复了原貌。

Four Great Regions. This is a massive complex of buildings forming a Tibetan-style temple. It was built in the Qianlong period, but was burned down by the Anglo-French Allied Forces in 1860. Reconstruction of these buildings began in late 1990s, and by now all the buildings have been restored.

四大部洲佛殿 为光绪年间在香岩宗印之阁原遗址上兴
建的，内供佛像。

Buddhist Hall of the Four Great Regions. This hall was
rebuilt in the Guangxu Period based on the Pavilion of
Fragrant Rocks and Ancestral Seals. A statue of Buddha was
worshipped inside it.

大殿主佛 殿内供三尊佛像，左为弥勒佛，右为燃灯佛，居中者为释迦牟尼佛。

Statues of Buddha. There are three statues of Buddha in the hall with Maitreya on the left, Dipamkara on the right and Sakyamuni in the middle.

十八罗汉 供于主佛左右两侧山墙边，相传是释迦牟尼的十八位弟子，受佛旨意常留人间，宣扬佛法。

Eighteen arhats. These eighteen arhats are on either side of the three statues of Buddha. Tradition has it that they were Sakyamuni's 18 followers, who remained in the human world to propagate Buddhism.

松堂　为一大庭院，院内古木扶疏。庭院东、西、北三面原有牌楼，除北面牌楼已恢复外，另两座仅存精美的夹柱石。

Hall of Pines. It used to be a large courtyard with many ancient trees. Originally there were archways on its east, west and north sides. Now only the archway on the north has been restored. The other two remain unrestored with their exquisitely carved pillar stones lying on their original sites.

宝琉璃塔　塔高16米，八面七级，全部用琉璃砖砌成。下为白石须弥座，上为镀金宝刹，顶部悬铜，风吹铃响，疑是梵声入耳。塔前立石碑，碑上用汉、满、蒙、藏四种文字刻着乾隆皇帝《御制万山多宝塔颂》。

he Glazed Tile Pagoda of Many Treasures. This pagoda is a seven-storeyed, eight-sided building over 16 etres high, inlaid from top to bottom with glazed bricks alternately of blue, green and yellow, on which are gravings of Buddha. It rests on a white stone platform and is crowned with a gilded pinnacle. From the top the pagoda are hung bronze bells, which produce a melodious sound in the wind. In front of the pagoda nds a stone tablet, on which is carved "Ode to the Imperially Built Pagoda of Many Treasures of Longevity ll" in Chinese, Manchu, Mongolian and Tibetan.

宁堂　原为后湖重要点景建筑。它傍水倚山，叠落而
，宁静清幽。1860年被英法联军焚毁；1996年按原样
建，现为颐和园园藏明清家具展馆。

anning Hall. Originally, this hall was an important building
the Back Lake area, nestling by the hill and facing the lake.
was burned down by the Anglo-French Allied Forces in
60. Rebuilt in 1996, it serves as an exhibition hall to
splay the furniture of the Ming and Qing dynasties.

苏州街　位于后湖中段，蜿蜒曲折300多米，建筑面积近
3000米。列肆于宫苑，始于汉代。苏州街和它上方的四大
部洲寺庙群形成了"以庙带肆"的商业模式。它以水当街，
以岸作市，共有64间铺面，14座牌楼、牌坊，8座小桥。

Suzhou Street. The street in the middle section of Back Lake
runs for over 300 metres along the lakeside, covering a
building space of 3,000 square metres. Building shops in the
imperial gardens started from the Han Dynasty. The Suzhou
Street here and the temple buildings of the Four Great Regions
formed a model of "promoting shops by temples". Along the
lakeside there are 64 shops, 14 gateways or archways and 8
small bridges, which looks like a street fair in south China.

云翰斋 店名源自民间老字号店铺，为文房四宝专营店。事实上，清代这里的店铺并不经销商品，而是设店装点街面，以供帝、后游乐。

Yunhanzhai Stationery Shop. This is an old-style shop for selling writing brushes, ink sticks, ink slabs and paper. But in the Qing Dynasty all the shops on the street did not sell any goods. They were just for the emperor and empress to visit.

云翰斋内景 店内为文房四宝，游客可用人民币兑换苏州街流通的古钱币，购买各店小商品，体验一下几百年前清人的乐趣。

Inside the Yunhanzhai Stationery Shop. All the writing brushes, ink sticks, ink slabs and paper in the shop are for sale. Customers can change the ancient coins that are circulated in the Suzhou Street and buy small commodities in the shops to experience the life of the people several hundred years ago.

北宫门　为颐和园北门，单檐二层庑殿式建筑。十八世纪下半叶，乾隆皇帝母亲常登楼观看门外前锋营骑兵习武，故又称阅武门。

North Palace Gate.　This two-storeyed gate is where Emperor Qianlong's mother used to come to watch the cavalry exercises of the Vanguard Battalion stationed outside the gate. It is also known as the Military Review Tower.

编　辑	宇　辰		
翻　译	振　儒		
摄　影	宇　辰	高明义	姜景余
	张肇基	姚天新	罗文法
	曲维波	王惠民	董宗贵
	刘思功	黄禄奎	何炳富
书名题字	溥　杰		

Editor: Yu Chen

Translated by: Z. R. Xiong

Photos by: Yu Chen　Gao Mingyi

　　　　　　Jiang Jingyu　Zhang Zhaoji

　　　　　　Yao Tianxing　Luo Wenfa

　　　　　　Qu Weibo　Wang Huimin

　　　　　　Dong Zonggui　Liu Sigong

　　　　　　Huang Lukui　He Bingfu

颐　和　园

宇　辰　编

振　儒　译

*

朝华出版社出版

意中艺广告有限公司制版

汇元统一印刷有限公司印刷

2001年6月（16开）第一版第一次印刷

ISBN 7－5054－0758－9/G.0213

05000